TANK MAN

HOW A PHOTOGRAPH DEFINED CHINA'S PROTEST MOVEMENT

by Michael Burgan

Content Adviser:
Hanchao Lu, PhD, Professor
School of History, Technology & Society
Georgia Institute of Technology

COMPASS POINT BOOKS
a capstone imprint

Compass Point Books are published by Capstone,
1710 Roe Crest Drive, North Mankato, Minnesota 56003
www.capstonepub.com

Editor: Catherine Neitge
Designer: Tracy Davies McCabe
Media Researcher: Wanda Winch
Library Consultant: Kathleen Baxter
Production Specialist: Kathy McColley

Image Credits
AP Images, 11, Jeff Widener, cover, 6–7, 14, 30, 33, 35, 40, 44, 48, 52, 59 (left),
Liu Heung Shing, 12, Mikami, 26, 58, Sadayuki Mikami, 8, Terril Jones, 42, Xinhua,
20, 29; Capstone, 39; Corbis: Peter Turnley, 5; Reuters/Tyrone Siu, 55, Sygma/
Jacques Langevin, 27, Sygma/Patrick Durand, 49; Courtesy of Jeff Widener, 46; Getty
Images Inc: AFP/Catherine Henriette, 23, 24, 31, 34, 36, 38, AFP/Jean Vincent,
19, AFP/STF, 17, AFP/Thomas Cheng, 10, Dario Mitidieri, 37, Hulton Archives,
21; Magnum Photos: Stuart Franklin, 43 (top); Newscom: Reuters/Arthur Tsang,
43 (bottom); Shutterstock: fstockfoto, 57, mary 416, 59 (right), Yu Lan, 56; Tim
Mantoani Photography, 51

Library of Congress Cataloging-in-Publication Data
Burgan, Michael.
  Tank man: how a photograph defined China's protest movement / by Michael Burgan.
  pages cm.—(Captured history)
  Includes bibliographical references and index.
  Summary: "Discusses the iconic photo of a lone protester, Tank Man, stopping a row
of tanks near Tiananmen Square during protests in 1989"—Provided by publisher.
  ISBN 978-0-7565-4731-8 (library binding)
  ISBN 978-0-7565-4787-5 (paperback)
  ISBN 978-0-7565-4793-6 (ebook PDF)
1. China—History—Tiananmen Square Incident, 1989—Pictorial works—Juvenile
literature. 2. Widener, Jeff, 1956– Juvenile literature. 3. Photojournalism—China—
Juvenile literature. I. Title.
 DS779.32.B87 2014
 951.05'8—dc23   2013031196

Printed in the United States of America in Stevens Point, Wisconsin.
092013   007773WZS14

TABLEOFCONTENTS

ChapterOne
CRACKDOWN

They came from the city and the countryside, more than 100,000 Chinese soldiers. On June 2, 1989, they ringed the city of Beijing, the capital of China. For almost two months, the city's Tiananmen Square had been the site of growing protests in favor of political and economic reforms. Now the military was ready to end the protests once and for all and restore order.

The first protesters to gather at the square had been students from Beijing universities. Then students from outside the capital joined them, and so did teachers and workers. At first the students only wanted to honor one of their country's leaders, who had died in April. But within days their tributes turned to protests against China's strict government. The Communist Party controlled the government and most areas of life in China, and no other political groups had a say in what happened. The students wanted to change that. As the protests went on, and the world's attention focused on Tiananmen Square, Chinese government officials debated what to do. Now they were ready to act.

The next day, June 3, several thousand of the troops began entering the city and heading to Tiananmen Square. As they moved forward, tens of thousands of Chinese people flooded the streets of Beijing, hoping to stop them. One young man called to the soldiers,

A sea of student protesters gathers in Tiananmen Square in early May 1989. The Chinese government ended the protest with a bloody crackdown one month later.

"You are the people's army. The students' movement is patriotic, and you mustn't use violence against it. Think about it." But the soldiers had orders to follow, and they continued their advance.

A young woman is caught between protesters and soldiers who were trying to remove her from the square.

At times during the day, soldiers clashed with the
protesters. The soldiers swung wooden sticks. They
also used cattle prods, which delivered electric shocks.
Some were accused of shooting rubber bullets, which

A HISTORIC SQUARE

Soldiers stood guard at Tiananmen Square after the 1989 protesters were silenced.

Several of China's most important historic structures are in and around Tiananmen Square, which is in the heart of Beijing. The oldest is the Gate of Heavenly Peace, which dates to the 1400s, though it has been destroyed and rebuilt several times. Notable buildings include a hall dedicated to Mao Zedong, the first leader of the People's Republic of China, the official name for the country.

Tiananmen Square was also the site of another protest led by college students. In 1919 thousands of them gathered to show their anger over the Treaty of Versailles, which had ended World War I. The treaty, the protesters thought, was unfair to China because it did not return some Chinese land to the country's control. The activity began on May 4 of that year, and it sparked more protests and calls for reform that became known as the May 4th Movement. The People's Republic of China later honored these early student protesters, who had helped awaken a desire for a stronger China. Some of the protest leaders also had helped promote communism in China—the form of government still practiced there today.

are designed to injure people but not kill them. Some protesters fought back by throwing rocks. Later others would use firebombs, which were made from bottles filled with gasoline.

Starting around 6 p.m., radio and TV stations began to announce that everyone must obey the martial law that was in force. The government had placed limits on people's actions about two weeks before, but many of the protesters had ignored the martial law. Now the military's presence meant the government was serious about enforcing its orders. The media warned that "the martial law army, police, and armed police have the power to use whatever means necessary to force [people] to obey." Similar announcements followed through the evening, but few people left Tiananmen Square.

About 10 p.m. the power behind the government's threat was unleashed. Gunfire erupted in parts of the city. Then thousands of soldiers, some in armored vehicles, headed for Tiananmen Square. Some fired real bullets, while others stabbed protesters with their bayonets. Instead of fleeing, some student leaders marched to the center of the square, to the Monument to the People's Heroes. A student later said, "We were ready to receive the butchers' knives in peace." Some students talked to an army officer, trying to arrange for a peaceful withdrawal. The students began to leave, but violence began again later just outside the square.

Some protesters fought back with firebombs and rocks.

They managed to set several armored vehicles ablaze. The remaining students chanted, "Long live the people" as they watched the soldiers carry out their brutal assault. As they moved forward, the soldiers removed the bodies of some of the dead, so no one would know how many people had been killed. Other dead bodies were burned on the spot.

Students set an armored personnel carrier on fire during the height of the protest.

The dead bodies of protesters lie among mangled bikes near Tiananmen Square early on June 4.

The dead included children and the elderly. One student howled with sadness and anger after seeing a protester killed. "Maybe we'll fail today," he said. "Maybe we'll fail tomorrow. But someday we'll succeed."

Before sunrise the Chinese troops had taken control of Tiananmen Square, though protesters remained in nearby

A couple takes cover at a Beijing underpass as tanks roll overhead on June 5.

Burned-out cars and trucks sat on many of the city's streets, a sign that violence had spread beyond Tiananmen Square.

streets. Gunfire could be heard in the area throughout much of June 4 as more soldiers in tanks and armored personnel carriers moved in. Burned-out cars and trucks sat on many of the city's streets, a sign that violence had spread beyond Tiananmen Square.

Gunfire still rang out in parts of Beijing on June 5. But to China's rulers, the assault on Tiananmen Square had been a success. Its troops had ended a protest that the leaders thought threatened their power. More tanks rumbled through the city, and late that morning a long column of tanks rolled along Chang'an Avenue. This major east-west route lies just north of Tiananmen Square.

Around Chang'an Avenue photographers and video camera crews recorded the column of tanks moving along the street. Suddenly a man in white shirt came into view, standing in the middle of the street. Amazingly, to many people watching, the first tank stopped just a few feet in front of the man. The tanks behind it stopped as well. Then the driver of the lead tank tried to move around the single figure blocking its path. But the man moved too, staying in front of it. The tank driver tried to move the other way, and again the man cut the tank off. The movement became an unlikely dance between man and machine.

The man then scrambled up onto the tank and said something to the men inside. Some people reported that he shouted, "Why are you here? You have done nothing but create misery! My city is in chaos because of you!"

After a few seconds, he was off the tank, and several men led him away. Those watching the scene did not know his name. But soon millions would know about his bravery and about his desire to stop the military from trying to squash free speech and protest in China. One of the photographers near Tiananmen Square that day took a picture of the lone figure halting the line of massive armored weapons on an empty street. This image of the "Tank Man," as he came to be called, was soon sent around the world. It became one of the most famous photographs ever made.

ChapterTwo
THE CALL FOR DEMOCRACY

The 1989 protests and the government's crackdown reflected the reality of life in China. In a country of more than 1 billion people, just a handful of leaders in Beijing controlled how people lived.

Decades earlier, Communists led by Mao Zedong had battled other Chinese for control of the government. The civil war was interrupted in the 1930s and 1940s when both sides fought the invading Japanese. But Chinese once again battled Chinese after World War II ended. And in 1949 the Communists won nearly total control of mainland China. Their opponents, the Nationalists, set up their own government on the island of Taiwan. Today their country is called the Republic of China.

Mao believed that communism would help most Chinese escape poverty and build a stronger country. Mao and his top aides saw the party they led as the source of all political power. "The Chinese Communist Party," Mao said in 1957, "is the core of leadership of the whole Chinese people." People had to join the party in order to gain good jobs or have political influence.

Under communism, just one political party controls the government—the Communist Party. The people cannot elect their leaders, as they do in democratic countries, such as the United States. The Communist Party also controls the economy, and private property is limited.

Mao Zedong led China's Communist revolution and then ruled the country with an iron hand.

The government in a communist country is sometimes called totalitarian—the Communist Party has total control over almost all parts of life. At times Communists use violence, or simply the fear of it, to stop citizens from challenging their rule.

Under Mao tens of millions of Chinese were killed as the Communists asserted their power and tried to build a modern country. People who were too old or too sick to work on building projects were denied food. Food shortages sparked by government policies meant to control agriculture added to the death toll. Then, during the 1960s, Mao launched what he called the Cultural Revolution. He thought the Chinese were drifting away from communism and the goals of their earlier revolution. The government began strictly enforcing its orders and imprisoned those who opposed them. More than a million people were killed during this time.

The Cultural Revolution showed that China's Communist leaders did not always agree on how to run the country. Some, like Mao, thought they should always remain true to the teachings of the founders of communism, Karl Marx and Vladimir Lenin. They demanded that the people do as they were told. Mao and his supporters were willing to imprison or kill those who challenged them. Over time these strict Communists were sometimes called hardliners.

Others were less strict about following communist teachings and Mao's ideas. These Communists were more concerned about building China's economy, and they were willing to give people a little more freedom. These leaders were sometimes called moderates or reformers. But they, like the devoted supporters of Mao, were not willing to share political power with other parties. The Communist

Mao and his supporters were willing to imprison or kill those who challenged them.

In the mid-1960s many students joined the Red Guards to support Mao's Cultural Revolution.

Party would remain in control, and people who worked for the government often got better treatment than average citizens.

After Mao died in 1976, the two groups of Chinese leaders struggled for control. In the end, moderates led by Deng Xiaoping gained the upper hand. Deng had

Deng Xiaoping was a powerful leader in China from the late 1970s until his death in 1997.

helped fight the revolution that brought the Communists to power. But during the Cultural Revolution, he had lost favor with Mao for being a moderate. With Mao gone, Deng led the way in ending government control over parts of the economy and promoting trade with other countries.

Even with these changes, some students began to protest government policies in 1986. They particularly wanted to be able to choose who would represent them in the People's Congress. They also sought better conditions on college campuses. Several hundred students marched to Tiananmen Square to voice their views on

THE CULTURAL REVOLUTION

A giant poster of Mao looms over children in Red Guard uniforms during the Cultural Revolution.

Believing that too many Chinese were ignoring the core beliefs of communism, Mao Zedong called on young people to turn against their teachers and others who had lost the spirit of the revolution. As many as 11 million young Chinese joined the Red Guards, a group that attacked anyone believed to be against the government. Well-educated people known as intellectuals were a particular target of the Red Guards. Many were forced to do hard, physical jobs instead of working as teachers or artists. Others were sent to prison. Schools shut down, and competing groups of Red Guards sometimes fought each other for power.

After three terrifying years, Mao finally had to bring in the army to restore order. When Mao died in 1976, his wife Jiang Qing and three Chinese leaders tried to continue the government's harsh policies. But this so-called Gang of Four was arrested, ending one of the worst periods in modern China's history.

January 1, 1987. Other students put up posters that said such things as "We will fight for democracy; China should work for the people, not for a small group."

During the 1980s Hu Yaobang had emerged as another reformer. For a time he led the Communist Party, though Deng kept ultimate control over the government. When the student protests began, Hu seemed to support their call for more democracy. At least other Chinese leaders thought so, and they soon forced him out of his position as party leader. Hardliners also took control of more parts of the government so the remaining moderates would have less power.

To Communist hardliners, Hu had betrayed the party by supporting calls for reform. But among students and others who wanted democracy, Hu was a hero. When he died of a heart attack April 15, 1989, students in Beijing began heading to Tiananmen Square to praise him. Some placed wreaths at the Monument to the People's Heroes. Several thousand students marched to the People's Congress two days later and presented a list of demands. Among other things, they wanted freedom of speech and the right to demonstrate against the government. The students also called for the end of corruption in the government, which let some officials use their power to gain wealth.

Student leaders met April 19 at Xinhuamen Gate in Beijing, outside the headquarters of the Communist Party. They wanted to place a wreath honoring Hu and to present more demands. Some chanted "Down with Li Peng," a

To Communist hardliners, Hu had betrayed the party by supporting calls for reform. But among students and others who wanted democracy, Hu was a hero.

Students place wreaths in front of a portrait of reformer Hu Yaobang in Tiananmen Square.

hardliner who held a top position in the government. A line of police confronted the students as a crowd of about 10,000 people gathered. Fighting broke out, with some students throwing bottles and the police beating them in response. A government order came for everyone to leave. The students left, but soon an even bigger crowd began to form in Tiananmen Square.

By that evening the crowd had doubled and included teachers from the colleges as well as students. Some spoke to the crowd about the need for democracy in China. Meanwhile, a much smaller protest was going on in the city of Shanghai.

During the next several days protests continued, with some students refusing to attend classes. Despite the threat of police violence or arrest, many more came out to Tiananmen Square, including more than 100,000 on the day of Hu's funeral, April 22.

In an April 26 front-page editorial, the official

Police tried to stop the marchers with barricades, but the protesters broke through.

government newspaper, *The People's Daily*, criticized the students, blaming the protests on a few troublemakers. The paper said the student leaders wanted "to sow dissension among the people, plunge the whole country into chaos and sabotage the political situation of stability and unity. This is a planned conspiracy and a disturbance."

The People's Daily article angered many students. They believed their actions were legal and nonviolent and that they were trying to improve life in China. They organized a protest that drew 150,000 people. Police tried to stop the marchers with barricades, but the protesters broke through.

The next big rally was on May 4—the 70th anniversary of the first major student protests in Tiananmen Square. Smaller protests also broke out in other Chinese cities. In Beijing, as they marched toward the square, protesters sang a song that called for "peasants, workers, soldiers, [to] unite together!" Others sang, "We seek democracy! We seek freedom!" Student leaders kept the protesters organized, and, seeking to avoid violence, the police mostly left them alone.

Chinese journalists joined the protesters May 4, demanding that they be allowed to print the truth. The media, like most parts of Chinese society, had strict limits on what it could do. The Communists wanted to control what the people learned about life inside and outside of China. In the days that followed, students marched to show their support for the journalists.

More than 7,000 students gathered on May 4 to rally for democracy in China.

Over the next few weeks, the students continued to demand that government leaders meet with them to discuss their issues. The government dragged its feet, and 2,000 students began a hunger strike May 13. They refused to eat and risked their health to draw attention to their calls for democracy. Some even refused water. The first strikers issued a statement that said "We will defy death to win life for the nation." The hunger strikers, whose numbers grew to 3,000, and their supporters lived in tents set up around the square. Others slept in the open under blankets. A large tent in the center of the square served as the protesters' headquarters. A generator

Protesters continued their hunger strike during Mikhail Gorbachev's visit to Beijing.

provided electricity that powered lights and equipment the leaders used to broadcast messages.

In the midst of the protests, on May 15, the Chinese government welcomed a special foreign guest: Mikhail Gorbachev, the leader of the Soviet Union. Like China, the Soviet Union was a Communist nation. But under Gorbachev, the Soviets were beginning to get their first taste of freedom, under a policy called *glasnost*, which means "openness." The new policy also affected countries in Eastern Europe that had been under Soviet control since the end of World War II. For the first time in decades, people were openly challenging their Communist governments, and Gorbachev was willing to give them the freedom to do so.

To the Chinese students, the changes in Europe were a welcome sign. They also knew Gorbachev's appearance with China's top leaders would draw international attention. About 150,000 protesters filled Tiananmen Square the day he arrived. Some held signs printed in Russian that praised Gorbachev, and others applauded when his car drove by. Chinese leaders did their best to try to keep the Soviet leader away from Tiananmen Square and the protesters. They did not want to draw extra attention to the ongoing trouble in their country.

Gorbachev's visit was short, and the protests continued in full force. More than a million Chinese came out to show their support for the protesters May 17. They included farmers, workers, and even soldiers. Meanwhile, Zhao Ziyang, a top government official, sent the protest leaders a written statement. He told them to stay calm and not use violence. He also said they were showing their patriotism by calling for change. He spoke to the students at the square May 19 and asked the hunger strikers to begin eating again.

Another Communist leader, Li Peng, also met with students. He was one of the hardliners who wanted to take strong action against the protesters. In private, he told Communist leaders, "We must end the situation immediately. Otherwise, the future of the People's Republic will be in grave danger." The more sympathetic

"We must end the situation immediately. Otherwise, the future of the People's Republic will be in grave danger."

Zhao Ziyang met with students in Tiananmen Square and urged them to begin eating.

Zhao was forced out of his government position and placed under house arrest. He lived comfortably after that, but he never enjoyed the freedom and power he once did.

With Li Peng leading the way, the government took more steps to ensure order. It declared martial law in Beijing in an attempt to end public protests and limit news coverage of events in the city. Chinese troops began to approach the capital, joining troops that had been sent to the region soon after the protests had started in April. The government was obviously preparing to use force if it could not persuade the students to peacefully leave Tiananmen Square.

Students put the finishing touches on their *Goddess of Democracy.*

A new statue appeared in the square May 30—the *Goddess of Democracy.* Using Styrofoam and plaster, art students had quickly built a version of the American Statue of Liberty that was 33 feet (10 meters) tall. But as the protesters continued to call for democratic change, China's leaders were preparing to end the protests once and for all.

A student protester called on soldiers to go home as crowds filled Tiananmen Square June 3.

On June 3 several thousand soldiers marched to Tiananmen Square. Using clubs and electric prods, they tried to break up the crowds. That evening the government publicly declared the military's legal right to use force, since martial law was in place. As soldiers stood on the edge of the square early the next morning, protest leaders asked the several thousand people there whether they should leave. Most seemed to want to stay, but the leaders finally told everyone they should go.

But even with that decision, the early morning hours of June 4 would see the greatest violence. And in the streets around Tiananmen Square, photographer Jeff Widener did his best to show the world what was happening.

ChapterThree
TAKING THE PICTURE

As a professional photographer, Jeff Widener traveled the world to photograph people and events. In the spring of 1989, he was working for the Associated Press, a U.S. company that provides the media with news and pictures. He was based in Bangkok, Thailand, when word came that he should head to Beijing.

The Tiananmen Square protests were already under way, and getting into China wasn't easy. Widener went to see Chinese officials in Bangkok to get the visa he needed to enter China as a journalist. The Chinese refused to give him the visa. So he arranged to get into the country as a tourist—after first telling U.S. officials he had lost his passport and needed a new one. The old passport was already stamped by the Chinese government from earlier trips to the country. Border officials would suspect Widener was a journalist, not a tourist, if they saw the old stamps.

Needing to play this game to get into China was not surprising, since the government wanted to control what the world saw of the growing protests. That meant restricting the number of foreign journalists in China and limiting what they saw. Widener had an extra reason to be concerned as he entered China. The AP had asked him to take photography supplies with him. If border guards found the supplies, they would know he had lied about being a tourist.

Students rest in the litter of Tiananmen Square as their protest continues.

But Widener made it past the guards and went to a hotel about 2 miles (3.2 kilometers) from Tiananmen Square. He rode a bike to get around the city and photographed the growing protests. He saw the students put up the *Goddess of Democracy*. There was, he later wrote, "an electrified feeling in the air of hope and excitement."

On the night of June 3, however, Widener felt the air of hope change to one of growing fear and anger. He watched protesters place barricades on Chang'an Avenue to halt the advancing troops. The soldiers moving in were

from outside the city, because troops based in Beijing had
refused to fire on the protesters. Moments later, Widener
saw an armored personnel carrier smash through the
barricades. He dropped his bike and followed the action
on foot. He photographed students holding rocks and
bricks and saw a burning armored personnel carrier
jerking down the street.

In the middle of a growing mob, Widener feared he
might be shot, and the mob closed in around him. He
shouted that he was American and held up his passport,
hoping to persuade the protesters to leave him alone.
A leader of the group calmed the crowd and, seeing

Jeff Widener's camera captured a burning personnel carrier that had rammed through a barricade.

Widener's camera, told him to photograph a dead soldier near the armored personnel carrier. He took one shot and prepared to take another. Suddenly, with the camera against his face, he felt an impact like a punch from a boxer. A rock had slammed into his camera. Its tough metal body, made of titanium, had absorbed most of the impact and most likely saved his life.

The blow left Widener with a serious head injury, and he was bleeding where his camera had struck his face. Dazed, he got onto his bike and rode past Tiananmen Square. He heard the army's machine guns fire and saw the red streaks of light the tracer bullets created in the

Soldiers leap a barrier to forcibly end the protest in Tiananmen Square.

night sky. He made it to the AP office in Beijing, where he spent the rest of the night. Meanwhile, back near the square, the army was carrying out its deadly assault on the unarmed protesters. The troops had orders to clear the square by 6 a.m. and then keep it clear.

Widener went back to his hotel in the morning. Injured and sick with the flu, he slept most of the day. The next day the AP told him to go back to Tiananmen Square to take more pictures. The Chinese army had taken control there. Widener was still sick and unsteady from his head injury, but he went. With his camera and film hidden in his clothes, he rode his bike through the streets. Burned

Protesters watch as soldiers occupy Tiananmen Square.

buses lined the way, and he could hear gunfire.

Widener and other photographers went to the Beijing Hotel. It was one of the tallest buildings near the square and would be a good place to photograph the activity in the streets. But getting inside the hotel was not easy. Only guests were being allowed in, and Chinese security men in plain clothes swarmed the lobby. Entering the hotel, Widener approached a young man who looked like an American college student. His long hair and a T-shirt showing the movie character Rambo were helpful clues.

"Hi, Joe, where you been?" Widener said. In a whisper, he told the young man he was with the AP.

Onlookers run away as an armed soldier threatens them near Tiananmen Square.

The man, named Kirk, realized that Widener wanted his help to get into the hotel. Kirk played along and took him to his room. He also told Widener what he had just seen when he was outside the hotel: A group of soldiers had fired on tourists. Kirk had been lucky to escape uninjured.

Widener went to the roof of the hotel to begin taking pictures. He saw tanks ramming into burning buses. Small carts carried dead and wounded protesters away from the violence. Troops going by the hotel sometimes fired warning shots into the air, and some of their bullets hit the building. After a taking a few pictures, Widener ran out of film and asked Kirk to try to find some more. Kirk left and

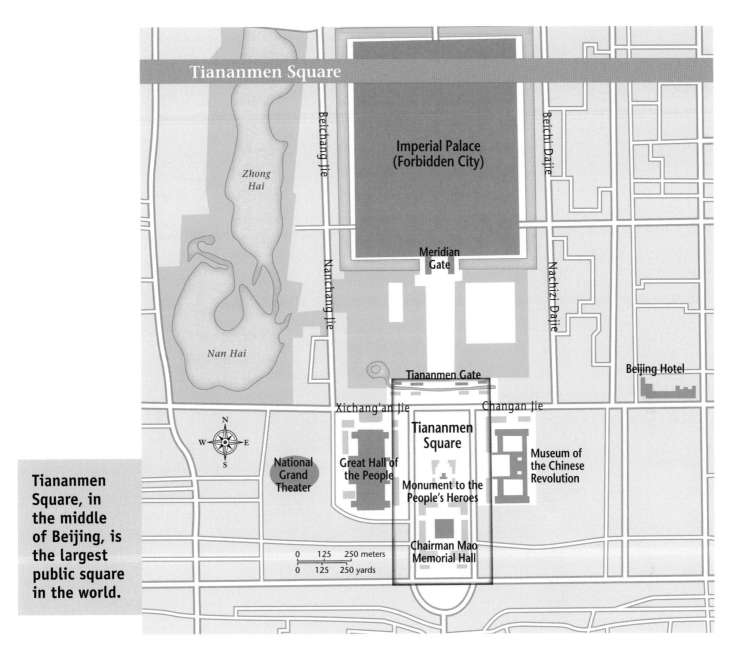

Tiananmen Square, in the middle of Beijing, is the largest public square in the world.

soon came back with a roll he had gotten from a tourist in the hotel. After taking more pictures, Widener, who had a bad headache, took a nap in Kirk's room. He woke to the sound of tanks in the street below. He grabbed his camera and went to the balcony. He saw Tank Man, holding shopping bags and staring down the approaching tanks.

Widener was concentrating on the tanks, and to him the man was a bother. "Damn it," he said to Kirk, "that guy's going to screw up my composition." Kirk saw the situation differently, and he shouted to Widener, "They are going to kill him!" Widener had been trained to capture on film the best and worst of human nature, and he wanted to photograph whatever happened next. But the action was too far away for him to get a good picture. He dashed from the balcony to the bed, where he had stored his gear. He grabbed a teleconverter, a device that would make the image look closer. He went back to the balcony and began to shoot, using the roll of film Kirk had found earlier.

Tank Man had climbed onto the lead tank. Just before Widener began to shoot, the protester jumped off the tank and stood motionless in front of it. Widener clicked away, but he worried about the kind of picture he would get. He wasn't using his regular film, and the camera's shutter had to be set to a slow speed. Taken from that distance, and using the teleconverter, the image might be blurry. But Widener would have to wait until the film was developed to find out. All he could do on the balcony was keep shooting. After several shots, people came and took the Tank Man off the street, and he melted into the crowd.

Widener shot his famous photo of Tank Man from a hotel balcony.

THE OTHER TANK MAN PHOTOS

Tank Man (far left, in the distance) waits for the tanks to approach in a street view of the famous confrontation.

Twenty years after the Tiananmen Square crackdown, *The New York Times* reminded readers that Jeff Widener was not the only photographer to capture Tank Man in front of the line of tanks. The newspaper identified three other news photographers who were on the scene and shot their own version of the events. Charlie Cole, who was on assignment for *Newsweek* magazine, took a picture that was similar to Widener's, though with Tank Man's bags more clearly visible. Cole said it was Tank Man who made the image, not him. "His character defined the moment, rather than the moment defining him." Stuart Franklin, on assignment for *Time* magazine, was shooting from the roof of the Beijing Hotel, like Cole. Franklin's shot is not as close, and it shows a burned-out bus in the background. Arthur Tsang Hin Wah, of the Reuters news service, took a photo of the scene a few seconds before the others. His shot has Tank Man and the tanks framed between two light poles. Once again, in the background, is the burning bus.

All three pictures appeared in print, and Franklin's was used as a poster that became popular around the world. The *Times* article led AP reporter Terril Jones to publicly reveal for the first time another picture of Tank Man. He took the shot on the street, not from above. Jones' photo shows the man waiting in the street as the tanks approach. But Jeff Widener's image remains the most famous Tank Man photo of all.

Photographer Stuart Franklin's Tank Man image (above) for Time magazine had the look of a painting. Arthur Tsang Hin Wah's image (left) for Reuters was cropped to frame Tank Man between towering light poles.

Widener knew he had to get the film to the AP office as soon as possible. He asked Kirk to take it on his bike. Security officials were not likely to think the young man was a journalist and try to stop him. Getting caught with the film would mean not only losing the shots but also being arrested. Kirk agreed, and he stuffed the rolls of film in his underwear and rode through the streets of Beijing. A few hours later, Widener called the AP office. The photo editor there told Widener the film had arrived and had been developed. The quality of the images wasn't great,

People on Beijing's Chang'an Avenue showed Widener a photo June 5 that they described as dead victims of the Chinese crackdown.

but some were good enough to send to AP's newspaper customers around the world.

Only years later did Widener learn Kirk's full name, Kirk Martsen, and the route he had taken to get the film to the office. On his bike, Martsen came upon soldiers with guns. Trying to avoid them, he began to cycle down side streets, and he got lost. So he went to the U.S. Embassy. Outside stood a Marine guard. Martsen explained about the film and asked the guard to make sure it got to the AP office. It did, and the picture of Tank Man was soon seen around the world.

Widener didn't know the fate of his photo and learn about its fame until the next day. He received messages praising him for the shot, which had been printed on the front pages of many major newspapers. Another photographer suggested he might win the Pulitzer Prize, the highest honor for a news photo.

Although he was a finalist, Widener did not win that prize, but he won continuing praise for taking what became one of the most famous photographs in world history. As Widener knew when he was shooting it, the shot was not one of his best technically. But he had captured a moment in a picture that had a great impact on the people who saw it. People knew that the peaceful protests for democracy in Tiananmen Square had turned violent. The Chinese government had killed its own citizens rather than let them freely speak for change. Yet even after that, one man had been brave enough to try to

The Chinese government had killed its own citizens rather than let them freely speak for change.

stop a line of tanks. He had risked his life and carried out his protest without violence. President George H. W. Bush praised the man's courage and said the image "is going to be with us a long time." And the photo was not just about the events in China. The idea of challenging the power of a government that hurts its own people could apply to many places around the world.

To some people, like James Barron of *The New York Times*, part of the power of the Tank Man shot was its simplicity. Earlier shots of the protests showed many people. This one showed just one man and a few machines. The scene, Barron said, also suggested the thoughts of the Chinese army during the protests, "with soldiers not sure when to press on and when to retreat." President Bush was impressed that the tank driver, a Chinese citizen, had not turned to violence. It was not easy for the soldiers to attack their own people.

While newspaper writers and others stressed Tank Man's bravery, Widener pointed out the bravery of another man during those troubled times in Beijing. As he later said, the American college student, Kirk Martsen, risked his life to get the photo to the world. "If not for all of his efforts," the photographer said, "my pictures may never have been seen."

Chapter Four

AN ENDURING IMAGE

While Jeff Widener was winning praise for his image, the Chinese people were dealing with the results of the June 3–4 massacre. For a time about 150,000 troops remained in and near Beijing, to make sure no new protests or violence broke out. Deng Xiaoping appeared on TV, after staying out of sight during most of the protests. He honored the work of the army for restoring order to Tiananmen Square.

Years later Li Peng claimed that, several weeks before the massacre, Deng had decided that the government had to "spill some blood" in and near the square to restore

Tanks gathered in Beijing following the brutal crackdown.

order. After the crackdown the government said "not one person" had been killed in Tiananmen Square and only 241 people had died elsewhere. People who had supported the protests thought the number was much higher, probably in the thousands. Both sides agreed that thousands more were wounded.

The government soon created a "most wanted" list and began searching for the students who had led the protests. Some hid in the country and avoided arrest. Many were able to sneak out of China and settle in the United States or Europe. Several student leaders were arrested, including Wang Dan, who was just 20 years old.

He served four years in prison. After his release, Wang spoke out again for democracy and was jailed again. When he was released a second time, he was exiled to the United States. He said years later that he felt sorry for the student protesters he organized who did not survive the massacre.

Jeff Widener's life was much different after he took his picture—for a time. He was invited to speak to hundreds of newspaper editors at a conference, an experience he dreaded because it made him very nervous. "I would have rather faced bullets in China," he said later, "than speak to that crowd." Besides appearing in newspapers, the Tank Man image filled two pages in *Life* magazine. Widener was thrilled—he had read the magazine as a child, when it was well known for offering the best photographs of the day.

But slowly life returned to normal for Widener. He resumed his career as a world-traveling photographer, and he now lives in Germany. He returned to Beijing in 2009 for the 20th anniversary of the event. He went back to the hotel where he had stayed, where he had hidden each time soldiers in the street fired their guns. He recalled how sick he had been the night before he took his famous picture. He said he had felt guilty for not staying on the streets, even after being hit with a rock. But balanced with that feeling, he said, was the "sheer terror of almost dying."

Widener also returned to Tiananmen Square. Changes there and in other parts of Beijing surprised him. Signs of capitalism were everywhere. The economic changes that began under Deng Xiaoping had continued, and they still

do today. China has the world's second-largest economy, worth more than $12 trillion. Only the U.S. economy is larger, and experts predict that China's will soon pass it. The enormous growth in wealth has filled Chinese cities with modern buildings and made people billionaires. Across the country millions of people are living better than they did before.

WHAT HAPPENED TO TANK MAN?

Who Tank Man is and what happened to him remain a mystery.

Who was Tank Man and what happened to him? Did he go into hiding? Was he arrested and executed? Is he still alive? Tank Man's identity and fate remain a mystery. Photographer Jeff Widener says the most commonly asked question about his famous photo is: "Whatever happened to 'Tank Man'"?

Shortly after the dramatic confrontation, a London newspaper reported that Tank Man was a 19-year-old student named Wang Weilin. But experts doubt the claim.

Timothy Brook, a professor of Chinese history, called the photo "the most extraordinary picture of the last half of the 20th century." He speculated about Tank Man's identity. "You could look at him as unusually brave," Brook said, "but he probably wasn't. He was probably just an ordinary person who was so disgusted at what he had seen for the last few days."

U.S. journalist Barbara Walters asked Chinese leader Jiang Zemin in 1990 whether the government had arrested and executed Tank Man. Through a translator, Jiang would not confirm that Tank Man had been arrested. But he added in English: "I think never killed." That was the last official statement on what happened to Tank Man. Today the mystery remains unsolved.

And Widener says that's fine: "I still think of him as the unknown soldier—the faceless guy who represents all of us."

The Tank Man photo shows that the "ultimate spirit of freedom will last longer than the strength of tanks and machine guns."

Yet in politics, little has changed since 1989. The Communist Party is still the sole source of political power. Corruption remains a problem; leaders still use their positions to get money for themselves and their families. And the government still tightly controls the news, trying to limit what the people learn about their own country and the world outside.

That control applies to the events of Tiananmen Square in 1989 and Tank Man. Most people who live in the People's Republic of China have never seen the famous photo in their own country. During the early 2000s, the creators of a public television documentary, *The Tank Man*, showed the famous picture to Beijing college students. They were 5 or 6 years old in 1989. The students knew nothing about the picture or the protests that came before it.

In 2012 an art museum in the Chinese city of Guangzhou displayed one of the Tank Man photos for several months in an exhibition entitled "Unseen Art." Still, most Chinese citizens who have seen the picture saw it while traveling in the West. Xiao Qiang was a graduate student in the U.S. when he saw it for the first time. The Tiananmen Square protests led him to take a more active role in politics and the fight for rights in China. To him, the photo shows that the "ultimate spirit of freedom will last longer than the strength of tanks and machine guns. ... [T]he Chinese Communist Party and its dictatorship will be gone. The men standing in front of tanks will stay."

The Chinese government still holds important events in Tiananmen Square, but it tries to shape what people learn about what happened there in 1989. When a Hong Kong publisher tried in 2010 to publish Li Peng's diary describing the Tiananmen Square events, the Chinese government threatened to sue him. (Large parts of the diary did appear on the Internet.) When the anniversary of the killings comes, people in China are not allowed to speak openly about it. The government even forbids the use of the word *tank* in postings on the Internet. On a recent anniversary of the crackdown, a small group of protesters came to Tiananmen Square. The police quickly arrested them.

Chinese leaders want the people to forget about true democracy and seeking reform. They want the people to forget about the 1989 protests—or never learn about them if they are too young to remember. But the world remembers the protests, and the lives that were lost at Tiananmen Square. And the image of a single person standing in front of a column of tanks will always remind the world of what happened in 1989. Tank Man will always stand for the courage of the people in demanding freedom even as they face their government's military strength.

Tens of thousands of protesters take part in a candlelight vigil in Hong Kong. The annual June 4 event remembers the 1989 crackdown on China's pro-democracy movement.

Timeline

1919

Students hold protests in Tiananmen Square, starting what is called the May 4th Movement

April 5, 1976

Major protest erupts in Tiananmen Square against the Gang of Four; it was prompted by Premier Zhou Enlai's death earlier in the year

September 9, 1976

Mao Zedong dies and moderate Communists begin to take control of the government

1949

Mao Zedong proclaims the People's Republic of China after leading a revolution that puts the Communist Party in power

1966

The Cultural Revolution begins, leading to the death or imprisonment of millions of Chinese

1987

Several hundred students march to Tiananmen Square to protest the lack of democracy in China

April 15, 1989

Hu Yaobang, a moderate who opposes corruption, dies; students go to Tiananmen Square to honor him

Timeline

April 19, 1989

The number of pro-democracy protesters in the square grows to 20,000

May 4, 1989

A huge rally marks the anniversary of the 1919 student protests

June 2, 1989

Protesters prevent Chinese soldiers from entering Tiananmen Square

June 3–4, 1989

The Chinese army forces the students to leave the square and fights protesters in the streets of Beijing, killing or wounding thousands

May 13, 1989

Students begin a hunger strike to protest the government's refusal to meet with them

May 20, 1989

Officials declare martial law

June 5, 1989

Jeff Widener takes his famous picture of the Tank Man, and it soon appears in newspapers around the world

2013

Tens of thousands of people gather in Hong Kong on June 4 in what is now an annual event to remember the 1989 crackdown

Glossary

capitalism—economic system that allows people to freely create businesses and own as much property as they can afford

communism—system in which goods and property are owned by the government and shared in common; Communist rulers limit personal freedoms to achieve their goals

corruption—willingness to do things that are wrong or illegal to get money, favors, or power

economy—system by which a country produces, distributes, and uses its money, goods, natural resources, and services

embassy—building where the government representatives of another country work

intellectuals—people professionally engaged in mental labor, such as writers and teachers

martial law—control of a people by a government's military, instead of by civilian forces, often during an emergency

People's Congress—part of China's government that has elected officials, but the officials hold no real power and simply agree to what Communist Party leaders decide

sabotage—to damage, destroy, or disrupt on purpose

Soviet Union—former federation in eastern Europe and northern Asia that included Russia and 14 other now-independent countries; also called the Union of Soviet Socialist Republics (USSR)

tracer bullet—ammunition that leaves a trail

visa—government document giving a person permission to enter a foreign country

Additional Resources

Further Reading

Heits, Rudolph T. *Communism.*
Broomall, Pa.: Mason Crest, 2013.

Langley, Andrew. *Tiananmen Square: Massacre Crushes China's Democracy Movement.*
Minneapolis: Compass Point Books, 2009.

Mara, Wil. *People's Republic of China.*
New York: Children's Press, 2012.

McCollum, Sean. *The Chairman: Mao Unleashes Chaos in China.* New York: Scholastic, 2012.

Population 1.3 Billion: China Becomes a Super Superpower. New York: Franklin Watts, 2009.

Internet Sites

Use FactHound to find Internet sites related to this book. All of the sites on FactHound have been researched by our staff.

Here's all you do:
Visit *www.facthound.com*
Type in this code: 9780756547318

Critical Thinking Using the Common Core

A Chinese student protester is quoted on page 9, saying, "We were ready to receive the butchers' knives in peace." What does that mean? How does it relate to the image of the Tank Man? (Key Ideas and Details)

There are basic differences between communism and democracy. What were some of the freedoms the Chinese students wanted that citizens of such democracies as the United States and Canada enjoy? (Key Ideas and Details)

Do you agree with the expert quoted on pages 46 and 47 who said the image of one person protesting against the tanks was more powerful than seeing a crowd of protesters? Why or why not? (Integration of Knowledge and Ideas)

Source Notes

Page 6, line 1: Nicholas Kristof. "Beijing Residents Block Army Move Near City Center." *The New York Times*. 3 June 1989. 11 Oct. 2013. http://www.nytimes.com/1989/06/03/world/beijing-residents-block-army-move-near-city-center.html?ref=tiananmensquare&gwh=064D0EADEB655EC6C292C1D9AE4649E0

Page 9, line 11: *Ming Pao News* reporters and photographers, Zi Jin and Qin Zhou, trans. *June Four: A Chronicle of the Chinese Democratic Uprising*. Fayetteville: University of Arkansas Press, 1989, p. 142.

Page 9, line 23: Ibid., p. 152.

Page 10, line 2: Ibid., p. 143.

Page 11, line 3: Nicholas Kristof. "Troops Attack and Crush Beijing Protest; Thousands Fight Back, Scores Are Killed." *The New York Times*. 4 June 1989. 11 Oct. 2013. http://www.nytimes.com/1989/06/04/world/crackdown-beijing-troops-attack-crush-beijing-protest-thousands-fight-back.html?pagewanted=all&src=pm

Page 13, line 27: "Newspaper Excerpts, The Tank Man." *Frontline*. PBS. 11 April 2006. 11 Oct. 2013. http://www.pbs.org/wgbh/pages/frontline/tankman/cron/excerpts.html#2

Page 16, line 17: Quotations from Mao Tse Tung. Marxists Internet Archive. 11 Oct. 2013. http://www.marxists.org/reference/archive/mao/works/red-book/ch01.htm

Page 22, line 2: Julia Kwong. "The 1986 Student Demonstrations in China: A Democratic Movement?" *Asian Survey*, Vol. 28, No. 9 (Sept. 1988), p. 974.

Page 22, line 29: Mok Chiu Yu and J. Frank Harrison, eds. *Voices from Tiananmen Square: Beijing Spring and the Democracy Movement*. Montreal: Black Rose Books, 1990, p. 16.

Page 25, line 3: *People's Daily* editorial, 26 April 1989. 11 Oct. 2013. http://www.tsquare.tv/chronology/April26ed.html

Page 25, line 18: Philip J. Cunningham. *Tiananmen Moon: Inside the Chinese Student Uprising of 1989*. Lanham, Md.: Rowman & Littlefield, 2009, p. 25.

Page 25, line 19: Ibid., p. 26.

Page 26, line 7: *June Four: A Chronicle of the Chinese Democratic Uprising*, p. 57.

Page 28, line 26: "The Tank Man." *Frontline*. PBS. Transcript. 11 April 2006. 11 Oct. 2013. http://www.pbs.org/wgbh/pages/frontline/tankman/etc/transcript.html

Page 33, line 6: Jeff Widener. "Shooting Tank Man." *Post Magazine. South China Morning Post*. 9 Sept. 2012. 11 Oct. 2013. http://www.scmp.com/magazines/post-magazine/article/1031945/shooting-tank-man

Page 37, line 11: Ibid.

Page 41, line 2: Patrick Witty. "Behind the Scenes: Tank Man of Tiananmen." *The New York Times*. 3 June 2009. 11 Oct. 2013. http://lens.blogs.nytimes.com/2009/06/03/behind-the-scenes-tank-man-of-tiananmen/

Page 41, line 4: Ibid.

Page 42, line 10: Ibid.

Page 46, line 3: "The Tank Man."

Page 47, line 2: James Barron. "Crackdown in Beijing; One Man Can Make a Difference: This One Jousted Briefly With Goliath." *The New York Times*. 6 June 1989. 11 Oct. 2013. http://www.nytimes.com/1989/06/06/world/crackdown-beijing-one-man-can-make-difference-this-one-jousted-briefly-with.html

Page 47, line 11: Patrick Witty. "Tank Man Revisited: More Details Emerge About the Iconic Image." *Time*. 5 June 2012. 11 Oct. 2013. http://lightbox.time.com/2012/06/05/tiananmen/

Page 48, line 11: Peter Foster. "Tiananmen Square memoir claims China decided to 'spill some blood.'" *The Telegraph*. 4 June 2010. 11 Oct. 2013. http://www.telegraph.co.uk/news/worldnews/asia/china/7803514/Tiananmen-Square-memoir-claims-China-decided-to-spill-some-blood.html

Page 49, line 1: "The Tank Man."

Page 50, line 9: Claire O'Neill. "What Comes After Tiananmen's 'Tank Man'?" National Public Radio. 4 June 2009. 11 Oct. 2013. http://www.npr.org/blogs/pictureshow/2009/06/tankman.html

Page 50, line 24: Jeff Widener. "Returning to Tiananmen Square." *Huffington Post*. 4 June 2009. 11 Oct. 2013. http://www.huffingtonpost.com/jeff-widener/returning-to-tiananmen-sq_b_211138.html

Page 52, line 6: "What Comes After Tiananmen's 'Tank Man'?"

Page 52, line 12: "The Tank Man."

Page 52, col. 2, line 8: "Barbara Walters asks Jiang Zemin 'What happened to the Tankman?'" YouTube. http://www.youtube.com/watch?v=njqLAv-wYeM

Page 52, col. 2, line 11: Jeff Widener. "How an Iconic Image Came to Be." *USA Today*. 4 June 2009. 11 Oct. 2013. http://usatoday30.usatoday.com/news/world/2009-06-03-chinaphoto_N.htm

Page 53, line 25: "The Tank Man."